MW00324010

SECRETS OF A BROKEN HEART

Secrets of a Broken Heart
5x8 First Edition Paperback
978-0-9984381-5-3
Published by Secret Midnight Press
Layout by Jason Turner
Copy editor: Alex Curnow

www.secretmidnightpress.com
www.Leemartens.com

Secrets of a Broken Heart

by Lee Martens

Tales of a broken heart

Ever since I can remember,
people have been labelling me
female. I will be remembered as
a something year old woman. A
woman died last night in a car
crash or because of a broken
heart, the papers will read.
These are the tales that
they will tell, wishes
whispered in the dark.

It's beginning to look like the end.

Modest sadness

A soft
knock
on the door.

I have been expecting you.

Tears
roll
slowly.

Temporary happiness

I wish I could
stay here
in this state of mind.

But I know
it's just a matter of time
until I go back.

Excitement is great
but it is not enough to sustain
a writer's brain.

For as much as I dislike it
I am addicted
to the feeling of pain.

I wrote this on my birthday

I said: "I miss you –
this week has been so long."
You asked me to explain
why my hours felt like days.

We talked about school and about
how I've been staring at a Word document
for days
but in all the messages you sent,
I never once heard you say
your heart has been aching for me
in the way my body falls apart
without your arms to hold.

I shouldn't have said anything at all.

Forever

Soft were his arms,
warm was his voice.
I would have stayed forever
had he given me a choice.

Gifted wisdom

1.
My dentist presented me with two
wisdom teeth on a tray.
"Want a souvenir?" he asked.
I said "no, thank you."

If you had asked me the same question
as my dentist back when you
took parts of me, I don't know
if I would have replied yes.

2.
Local anaesthesia;

You kissed me on my mouth and my
body went numb. I couldn't feel a thing,
couldn't even hear a sound when you took
pieces of my heart and never came back around.

The night

I am the night;
you only wish for me occasionally.

Permanent memories

Do you remember that time you wore
a red T-shirt and sat with your back
against my white wall? You left a pink
stain and never apologised – I think you
liked leaving a permanent mark in my room.

I wish I could tell you that it is almost gone
now. I tried everything to erase it. Some
water and many cleaning agents. The
sun helped too, shining through my
bedroom-window every once in a while.
I poisoned and burned whatever was left.

You are almost gone now; how does that
make you feel?

Valentine's Day

I read your letter again today,
the one you used to break up with me.
It was a week before Valentine's Day
when I first received it. We had been
together for almost two years.

It has been a few years since
but one sentence still hits me hard.
You wrote, and I quote:
"I want to love you forever, to always
like you, but I can't. I just can't."
There were many more words in the letter,
but none to make it better.

I have tried too, to love myself forever
and have found that it is very hard to do,
so I don't blame you.

Power outage

I wasn't scared of the darkness
until you left. This is
the absence of light and now
I feel the hole in my heart more
than before. More than before
the air feels cold. The people
have gone to sleep and not even
you are awake when I fail
to close my eyes. You used to be
only one call away. Stumbling
through the dark, I have lost
the way in my own home.
There are clothes on the floor
that I trip over. I wasn't scared
of the darkness until you left.
What if something happens now?
Who will I call? Who will hold
my hand when I trip and fall?
When my heart gives out,
who will restart it? The darkness
swallows me and I do not know
how to be without fear anymore.

Who am I to you?

Who am I to you if I am not the sea,
not the ocean, not the see you soon?

Not the land you stand upon,
the arms welcoming you home.

I am not the earth after flight,
the kiss goodnight.

When we say our goodbyes,
for how long will that be?

When will I see you again

if I am not the end of the adventures,
not the bend in the road?

I am your friend
but I wish I could be more.

Unrequited love

I can create so much, needing
only a pen and a piece of paper.
I can write about the ocean,
how it opens and closes doors.
You have seen nothing like it before.
I can write stars from scratch,
add a bit of sunshine and
have everybody smile. And yet,
I cannot create love. Cannot
even replicate the feeling.
The need for arms around me
goes unfulfilled. I know
I have love in different forms.
It is all around me. I love
my friends, as long as they
will have me. I love my family
and they love me. But nothing
comes quite close to that
ghostly feeling of you.
Goosebumps where arms
used to touch, chills
every time I enter a dark room
alone. It is night and I
am by myself, wondering
where it is that I am home.

Unrealistic television

On those dating shows on TV,
whenever someone gets sent home,
they say "I guess I just didn't show
enough of myself" and I wonder
what it is like to have that kind
of confidence. When people
break up with me,
it always seems to be
because I showed too much.

Laughter

I love that time
we laughed together.
It was simple,
no wires under grass
no paths between stars.
Just light in my eyes
and your hand right here
in my palm.

I miss the way
we are together.
It was simple,
but now it is
simply not.

Watch where you're going

I learned two things yesterday,
when I walked into a wall
head first.

One; watch where you're going,
life hurts when you only
live it inside of your mind.

Two; you can't blame still objects
for your pain. He left a mark
but was never in the wrong.
He came with no surprises.
He stood still and you knew
that all along. You both wanted
different things, if only you
had watched where you were going.

Hopeless wishes

I wish I was yours
but you are
everybody's favourite.

It is all okay

I sent you a message yesterday
when I thought everything was still okay.
I didn't hear back, not even today.
I pretended that everything was fine
because what else do I tell my friends?
You didn't tell me where you went.
You didn't even say that you were leaving.
Not this time, at least. And I don't know
what I would have said if you did tell me.
Could I have talked you out of it?
Could I have made you stay? I tell my friends
that I am okay because I am still living
in the moment of yesterday, when you were just
a message away and not across the sky
somewhere I cannot reach.

Don't be gone

People are saying that you left
the earth before your time
and I am left wondering
if that is true.
You never said goodbye.
I know that you were tired
but where have you gone?
What happened to your eyes
and the songs you used to sing?
Can I be selfish
and ask for one last thing?
Please come back and tell me
that it is not true, that you
have not been united with the moon
that when the sun shows
and tomorrow begins
your eyes will open and
you will let hope in.

What's next?

Restless

This is life and this is you,
scared eyes wandering around a dark room.
Where will your next step be?
Where is it safe for your feet to land?
There are hands reaching out,
people that know the way,
but in the back of your head
you can still hear a voice say
that your touch is poison,
so you move along,
hoping that when you eventually fall
there will be someone to catch you.

Identity crisis

The sadness spills out of me.
My identity on the floor,
feet slipping with every step I try to take.
I do not know who I am.

Who am I if I am not your daughter,
not your partner, not your friend? Alone,
I have no ground to stand upon.
Every day is a swim in the open sea.

Too soon

I was going to create something
make something out of the chaos.
But I stepped on the ice too soon,
neglected it room to grow.

Head underwater, sunk right in,
cracked the foundations.
Removed my safe land,
nowhere to go, nowhere to stand.

Fallen stars

I am the crash
of the night.
All of my fears collided
and my friends fell
like shooting stars;
I tried to wish for the fall
to end but I cannot
mend water.

Disappointment

On the weather forecast, they said
there was going to be a heavy
storm today, so I got ready.
I bought frozen pizza and
cans of soup. Got my blanket
from the closet, collected
my favourite books. But
the storm never showed.

It is that kind of
disappointment I feel
when my brain tells me something
terrible is about to happen
but the blow never hits. It is
not like I want to be knocked
down by the wind but
what do I do now
with all the time I have and
with the bright sky overhead?

My best

My mum has always said that if I do
my best, I can achieve anything.

But when my best is put to the test,
others are better and I cannot get any rest.

Insecurity

So many people
that say I have talent;
I don't hear a sound.

My mind speaks louder
insecurities nestling in
my brain, here to stay.

Poetry is just words to paper,
minutes in ink and I think
that this is all I am.

Late night fear

It is late at night again and
I do not know why I am
awake to see the time change.
Can I stop the clock and
mute my brain?

I gave my happiness away
during the day, handed
my smile to strangers on the street
and my heart to friends that said
they would not leave me –
I am scared they will.

And now, I wonder
what is left. Am I anything
more than a chest filled with fear
and a mind too frightened
to give in to the night
and the ending days?

Outside

Have you ever felt like you were looking at your body
from the outside?
Sometimes I feel like I can see myself on the floor,
just a heap of clothes.
A heavy soul that it couldn't support.

Other times my skin feels like a weight that has been
put on me.
An unbreakable layer of something no one wants to
see and I am crumbling underneath.
Or is that just me and my insecurity?

Growing up

I was born with hungry eyes,
wanting to understand the works
of both the heart and
the brain. And I
have a lot to say.

But I grew up quiet and shy,
hiding behind books and paper.
Trying my best to fit in
but always sensing that
unspoken friction between me
and the rest.

Now I am 22 but I often
still feel like that little girl.
That is when the pages remain
unfilled and my voice unused.
I am so small, who would
even listen?

Skin

There was something poetic about his skin,
the way it seemed to sing words from his heart.
I wish my body felt like that.

Instead it's just rubber,
something to protect my soul but
nothing to show how I feel.

My body is the enemy

My body is the enemy and I
am sleeping on foreign ground.
My eyes are taped shut
and there is no sound
but the ragged breaths I try to take.

During the day I fake happiness
and sometimes it works.
Sometimes I feel the smile
in every part of my body.

But at night there is nobody.
There is only this shell
that I must call home.
Only this overgrown piece of skin
that lends itself to the fear within.

If you are not living,
you are dying and if you are neither,
you are lying to yourself.

I wish I could silence my mind
and find a quiet place to rest
that isn't in this panicked chest
of mismatched heartbeats.

Building safety

Where do you go
to hide away when
you do not feel safe
in your own body?

I write poems
to build myself
a new skin, one
that I won't die in.

I do not control my heart,
do not control my lungs.
I cannot tell them to stop
or to start.

So I take my mind in hand
and write myself a beat
and fresh air to breathe.
Here is to new hope.

Too much space

Whenever I think of love,
I think of how much space
my body takes up.
I think that that is why
I use words so much,
to create a front,
a place between us where words fly
and I do not need to be.

I take up too much space.

My friends always say
that I am small
as they are very tall
but somehow that feels
like a lie, like I managed
to beat the rules of science.

My body feels like a burden
as it holds together all of my darkest
thoughts and it still only shows
a smile. My body does not feel
like mine. It betrays me
when I feel sad and the heartbeat
starts racing or when I am scared
and suddenly I cannot breathe.
When tears prevent me from seeing
the sun or when my mind outruns
my lungs. I take up too much space
or I just crave for someone to say
that I fit perfectly in their embrace.

Take my love

I wish my skin could feel
as soft as his sweater,
that all of my tears could just
dissolve in the dimples
of my cheeks but my mind
seems to need more.
This body never feels like
it is enough. It is not a home.
I am scared of dying so
every day I fear my skin
will cave in, that all it holds within
will take over and start to fall apart.
My heart is not safe here,
so please take it.
I want you to be happy.

Memories

I went into an art museum and thought,
this is the only way I'll ever be in here.
My footsteps on the floor,
not my words on the walls.

It's the same with you.
I am only in your memory
with my hand on your arm,
not my kind words whispered in the dark,
not my wishes when we're apart,
not my heart in your head when I am dead.

I am only remembered when I am there.

Know me

A hundred new faces
and still no one knows how
to say my name.
Fifty conversations today
and the words ran dry
as rain betrayed my eyes.
All my life, I've wanted
for people to know me
but it's hard within limited time.
And I do not even know
myself anymore, not outside
the doubts that creep back in.

Where does the sadness end
and where do I begin?

Lack of structure

My mind is racing and I cannot
keep up. Yesterday someone
complimented me on being
a fast typist. They were quite in shock
by how fast my fingers moved
across my keyboard and I said
'well, I had to do a typing
course as a child' but to be
honest, that is not the real reason.
The thing is, my body had to get
equipped to deal with my mind.
My hands learned to type at the
speed of light and still they are always
one step behind.
I cannot keep up. My brain had to learn
too so here I am studying for a degree
in how to structure stories for TV
so that I can deal better with the downfall
of words because my eyes are a cracked
screen that blur the lines between
beginning, middle and end and that would
confuse anyone listening. I am sorry.
I am not always making perfect sense,
not even to myself. I wish I could just
go to sleep.

The exhaustion after the fight

I wish you could see it like you see a broken arm,
the way my heartbeat races. My smile takes me places
but my breath does not come easy and my feet
are hesitant. I want to stay in bed but I also want out
of this head. I am out of my mind with thoughts chasing
my dreams, lungs refusing to breathe, arms failing
to catch me.

This is the exhaustion after the fight
and I wish I could convince myself
that it is going to be alright.

Exhaustion

I am so tired that I told my neighbours
about my week. Told my cats
about my sheep. How they could
creep up to them in the dark.
Black against white. I told my
shadows to write something else
than letters to myself each time
that I feel down. I told my mind
to go to sleep but it has never been
one to follow commands. The heart
does what it wants.

Most alone

I feel most alone at night,
when my dreams remind me
that you are not by my side anymore.

I feel most alone just before sleep
when I need to say goodnight to someone
so I whisper it to the walls.

I feel most alone in the morning
when I tie my shoelaces knowing
that my feet won't walk towards you.

I feel most alone when I'm with friends
and their conversations never seem to end;
I have left my voice with you.

Is there a way to cure this ache?
Right now I am not even sure
who it is I miss, just that there is a hole,

And I feel most alone.

Loneliness

Sometimes I wonder
if I am still here.
How many people need to forget
my name for me to disappear?

Three people misspelled it today,
others didn't know how to say it
and somehow that feels like
a summary of my existence.

How many people do I need to meet
to find someone who understands?
Who will take my hand and
show me the world.

Depression #1

On days when I feel depressed,
I think of all the poems
I have in my head,
of how they will all go
to waste because my thoughts
are racing
and I cannot
keep up.

Depression #2

The pain goes deep, all the way
from my lungs to my feet
trying to get out of bed.
I have been feeling like this for weeks.

Gone are the days of feeling other things
deeply; no butterflies in my stomach,
only a slight rumble when I haven't
eaten anything all day.

I wish I could say something, find
my voice and tell my mind
to snap out of it but I am left
without the power to speak.

My body still flinches when somebody
tells me I am beautiful because of
how the last guy treated me so why
would I say it to myself?

I looked online for self-help tips
but I can't remember the last time I truly felt
okay; the way back is so unfamiliar
that I stumble with each step.

The pain goes deep
so I'll just go back to sleep.
In dreams I might find
the opposite side of feeling too much.

Late night thoughts

At night I think back to all the conversations
I had that day. All the things I didn't say.
Everything I should have said but
couldn't formulate into sentences
because my mind is always a step behind life.
Words move at the speed of light in my head
but my mouth is unequipped and stumbles
and falls when I try to run.
Now I'm awake and whisper the words
to the ceiling. There is so much
about me that you will never know.

A conversation

The words are under a bench.
We are sitting there,
just staring at the clouds
and at the people that walk by.
You ask me how I am doing
and I say I am fine.
We talk about everyday life,
about the people we have met
and what we had for breakfast.
Every sentence is made out of
carefully picked words,
none of the ones we'd have to bend
down for, because god forbid
they see your skin move,
your layers unfold.
None of the words we'd have to dig up,
because no one should see the dirt
under your nails. We tiptoe
around the world.
We are sitting on a bench,
smiling through the hurt.

Let's go

I wish that I could disappear
but also that someone
would notice,
that just before I completely
slipped away, they'd
knock on my door and say
"let's go watch a film,
we can disappear together
in the lives displayed
on the screen, even if it
is just temporarily."

Saddening song

Sing me a saddening song because
the world has crashed down around me
and I don't know where I went wrong.
Have the notes bring my eyes to tears
and block my throat, I have no use
for words. The world
collapsed and I do not know
which step did it, which moment
of pressure was finite and final.
Hold me in your arms while I cry now.
I need you to. I can't get off the floor
of my bedroom but the carpet
is cheap and used. My back hurts.
My head has had enough.
Get me back up.

A life of small complaints

When I was younger, I used to
complain a lot. I think it was
the only way I knew to say
that I was not doing okay.

My eyes became sensitive
to the sun; I blamed the clear skies
for the tears in my eyes.

Every time it rained I would say
"man, I wish I lived somewhere else,"
and that was true.

When I had nothing to do I would
say that I was bored but I felt
myself prisoner of my mind.

All goodbyes became sad songs,
morning wishes for more time
and all I said was 'I am tired'.

I am older now and express
my feelings through poetry, but
most poems you will never see.

They are laced with bad days
and complaints and I wish to be
a happier me.

A bouquet

I wish I could bundle
all my emotions up
into a bouquet of flowers.

I haven't forgotten about you.

It's back

Look! There it is!
The feeling you missed,
the songs that went,
the smile that left,
everything you thought was gone;

There it is! Happiness
returns, even when you think
the curtain is closed
and the sky fell

Tomorrow will tell;
happiness
is back.

Silly dreamer

Silly dreamer,
can't seem to stop.
Your mind drew you a ceiling,
your heart just keeps going up.

Yellow nails

The yellow paint is starting to fade,
the stars seem to be hiding
and the moon is out of sight.

I am trying to fight the emptiness,
the grey that is taking over inside
and destroying all the light colours.

I put on a song and try to sing along,
because if I can still sing
there must still be a heartbeat within me.

A smile might help too so I try
to find happiness in other people
and attempt to mirror their mind.

Tonight will still be bad and it
will still hurt, but I've seen hope
and I've heard that that lasts.

You're not welcome here

My anxiety is not who I am.
We might seem friendly because
it follows me around wherever I go
but my heart is not its home.

A reminder

Remind me to never fall
for the dark, I know
there is light in my heart.

We always want what we
don't have; there is an
endless longing in my chest.

But I won't fall for the dark,
there is
light in my heart.

Upside-down

You know what? I have
decided that the world
looks better upside-down.

I would like all frowns
to be turned into smiles
and all of my problems
faded into the sky.

Flowers

Nobody sees sunshine in the midst of a storm,
but the people that say they
hate the rain are wrong

Look how many flowers grow from seeds,
how many blades of grass
battle from the ground on up

Look at the water from your eyes
and know that this
is what is making you feel alive

And yes, after the storm has passed
brighter days will come
and the sun might show

But know that it is okay
to have the rain
grow flowers on your cheeks

Sweet dreamer

Sweet dreamer,
the stars are yours now.

It is dark out
and the night will always be
just a few hours away
but the stars
are yours now.

Small poem

This is a small poem,
not many people have
heard its name. It
likes to stay away,
hiding in the corner
of the page.

Wishing

Let me tell you a story,

It starts like this: there was once
a little girl who had a great big
wish. Every night before she went
to sleep she'd repeat
the wish inside her head,
hoping it would follow her
into her dreams.

The middle part of the story
is less hopeful and might even
be seen as sad,
but as time has shown
and life has learned,
hopes grow when they are
repeated in a dreamer's mind
so don't you worry
sweet little child.

How does the story end?
I do not know yet,
but I am excited for
the road ahead
and still every night
before sleep captures
my mind, I wish
for that future
and let my dreams
follow my heart.

Tragedy

Love is not a tragedy.

It is a sad song,
the one you cannot stop singing;
one day it'll lift you up.

A universe

I am surprised by my own mind;
it has so many undiscovered corners.

This is up for grabs

"There is a story here," she said.

"There is a story here.

I feel it in the air but
it's just too far away to touch.
And even if I could reach it,
I could not keep it.

It is not mine.

I can only try
to mirror its words,
catch its ways on paper

and hope that the reader still
believes that it is sincere."

There is a story in my pen

There is a story in my pen,
a voice in my ink that I think
the paper might like to meet.

We'll see if they can get along.

The one, you are

You are the
one day you(r)
will-power to
see(k) more new
dreams are just
you are the
hope is special.

Happiness, one day at a time, one

Some days you tell yourself
that you are not beautiful.
You look at your soul
and see only its flaws, only its
mistakes, but you know what,
life is about give and take,
bruises and stitches.

Your heart black and blue
but it is still you and there
is a beat, there is life.
By definition that means light,
the absence of darkness
and maybe you're right,
maybe light does not equal
happiness, but you will
get there, one day at a time.

Happiness, one day at a time, two

Sorry I forgot about you
for a while, life
got in the way and I know,
that shouldn't be an excuse.

Happiness should come first,
but tell that to my anxiety,
let my depression know too,
speak to the tears and the fears.

And the long nights during which
I am alone in my room,
wondering if I have the strength
to take a shower.

Happiness should come first
but I do not know if I
have that magical power
to make the rest come second.

Vocabulary

My poems always seem to revert
to the same form, using only
a set amount of words.
I am a master of this language
when it comes to my heart but
I still find it hard to order drinks
at a bar. I can't describe the weather
or what constitutes the beat that brings
air to my lungs. Biology's terms
have always been a mystery to me
and my mind cannot describe
all the things my eyes see.
Words fail me more than they are
at my side. I can never seem to catch
enough, can never seem to know them all.
It is the blessing and the curse
of someone who was born on foreign land
and has had to write their youth
in unfamiliar hand.

Dreaming distraction

I want to see the world.
I want to swim across oceans
and jump into the sky.
I want to be one with the stars
and say hi to the moon.
But while I am thinking all these things
I am just sitting here, in my room.
My eyes wander across the screen,
thinking of futures yet to be seen.
I should go and do some work
but my mind won't cooperate.
Every time I blink I jump
and am in a different universe.
My feet don't touch the earth
anymore, and I don't want them to.
I just want to dream, even if it is
with my body in this room.

Regaining focus

Honey, you are so pretty that
the ground cannot get enough of you.
Your tears are the water to the earth,
your red eyes the sun to the flowers.

I know that you like to help,
but remember that the sky
needs you just as much.

Being me

I think most people that have met me
this year have seen both sides
and I take pride in that,
because it is hard
to show emotion,
hard to show fear.

You

You give your words away easily or so it seems.
I know that that is not true but you
make it seem like speaking is simple,
almost as if it is not worth much.

You get on a stage and rush
through your poetry,
leaving no room for interruption,
no time for silence.

I recognise that in me,
mumbling when someone asks for
my name, my hands shaking
when I write poems at night.

The words never feel right
so I give them all away,
racing to get enough time
to do so, there is too much to say.

When a poet gets on a stage,
most people see confidence,
but I am looking at my running mind,
my heartbeat in my throat.

There is hope that words will
save you but just in case
these are not the right ones,
I'll race through my vocabulary.

Maybe someday I can stand there too,
like you,
and we can both let go of that insecurity
of not being good enough.

Writer's block

I used to always know
what to write, I would
sit down at night and
get rid of all the words
that were lingering in my
mind. Words come
slowly
now and
each one
I have to fight for.
Some days
I am a writer,
other days
I just
feel.

Coin

I keep a coin in the deep pockets of my coat.
It is a secret to all but one person I know.
I hold onto it in my left hand whenever I go outside,
silently telling myself: it is going to be alright.
It twists between my fingers,
spinning to the songs my heart sings.
Confined to one pocket-sized object,
hope is a wonderful thing.

Goodnight

Goodnight to the sky,
it is time to go to sleep,
but go out with a fire.

A sunset so bright
to remind me that the light
is strong enough to return.

The moon is dreaming too

The moon sits in a circle,
drinking tea with the stars.
Telling stories about the future,
hoping dreams forever last.

Something new.

Mornings

This is new. The brewing hope
during breakfast after I have had
little sleep. The sun
on my skin and the beginning
smile at the corners of my mind.
This is new,
and it starts with you.

Falling in love #1

You have said more words to me
in dreams than awake.
I've made you laugh,
I've watched you smile.
You held my hand tightly
and for a while
life was sweet.

Meeting you eyes open soon
and I'm hoping you have dreams too.

A night like this

Your arm rests around my
shoulder. My head is pressed
into your chest. This is
safety and me
at my best.

Your voice

There is something funny
about your voice,
the way it echoes in my mind.

It is ironic almost,
how the sound I have always
wanted to hear makes me go
speechless.

How the words suck away
the thoughts I had until
all I can do is stare at you
and nervously giggle,
cheeks blossoming
and dimples growing.

Quiet love

He is someone who loves.
It is so much of what he does
that it becomes so much
of what he is.
It is his nature to love,
which is why the strain goes unnoticed,
the tears are unseen.
He is love
so when love is not there,
who is he?

She is the opposite kind of love,
the quiet love, the one you only
notice when you feel her heartbeat
through her chest. She does not
need to hear the words, she can
see them in his eyes. She does
not need for him to answer her
questions, all she ever wanted to
know fits inside their embrace.

This is the kind of love
he comes home to,
when he feels empty after having given
his heart away so many times
to different people
during the day.
It is okay; she will stay.

Magic

This is where dreams
come true. Right here
with you. There is magic
in the air today and
I know you feel it too.

Growth

It started raining at five in the morning. That's when she woke up, water still plastered to her cheeks. He was always leaving, and had left once more the night before. Not a word was spoken, but she felt it in the silence. Where there is room for improvement, there is also space for emptiness and that is all the rain filled. There was nothing to wash away, simply her tears to disappear from the eyes of the world. She was standing in the middle of the road. It didn't matter; no cars passed at this time of day or they just never seemed to be going her way. Been living here for a year and still she does not own an umbrella because why keep from catching the rain? Why stop from feeling? Quivering in the cold, that's when life comes back in. Goosebumps on skin. It's only the beginning and soon she will know that this is where flowers start to grow inside the empty spaces of her heart. The pain is a new start.

Hotel

I sometimes wish my heart was a hotel.
One with a clear guest list so that when
it is full, I can say no at the door.

But my heart is more like a crowded city.
It has got hotels too, nice places for you to stay
but on your way you will probably get lost
in my love. I am so sorry.

The kind of notes I'd
leave around our house

I wish I could spend my days inside your mind
and my nights inside your embrace,
for as much as I don't understand life,
I do get you and you
have got me.

Growing happiness

I tried to grow flowers on my chest,
held on to all the things I thought I needed.
The ground, the water from my eyes,
the stones to surround it.
But happiness grew heavy
and never fully blossomed.

I have decided that it's better
to get it off my chest,
write away the yesterdays
and the sad ways of coping.
I am hoping to learn
to grow flowers in my mind
by only holding on
to the sunlight that radiates
from your smiles to your eyes.

Valentine's Day #2 /
Taking back control

I remember being 14.
My best friend had her first kiss.
They held hands in school hallways.
Meanwhile I focused on my breathing.
It was always a bit too rapid but no one noticed.

I remember being 16.
The night before Valentine's.
I wondered if someone ordered a rose for me at
school, or if I'd find a secret note in my locker.
The next day my friends and I were bundled around a
desk, trying to figure out the handwriting on a note
my friend had gotten. My pockets were empty,
but my head still filled with dreams.

I remember being 18. I stayed up until two am
every night talking to a boy. I told him I liked him.
He said he felt the same but he always forgot
Valentine's Day. Dating him for two years
was a waste of wishing space.

I am 23 and it's the night before Valentine's.
I write myself secret love notes on my phone.
Taking back control.

Second-hand happiness

My friends are really happy
and do crazy cool things.
I get to watch and think
one day, we will reunite
and I can be as happy as they are.
Until then, their smiles
are my sunshine and
their hopes and dreams
my reason to get up in the morning.
I'd like to see all of their
wishes come true.

New faces

There are lines on your face
that I have never seen before.
Your mind works in curious ways.
It's what I like most about
meeting a new person,
about seeing a new face.
There are so many things to discover,
so many lines to see move when they smile.
The world is ours now. There are wonders out there
to find, new smiles to see and
hearts left to touch and to be touched by.
Don't close your eyes.
Read between the lines.

Grateful

Happiness is when you tell someone
you love them and they say
'thank you'. Because although
'I love you too' is nice,
there is so much beauty in
'thank you'. It is knowing
that you have helped someone
see their value. I will never stop
trying to make people smile.

Happy alone

As a child I once made
a drawing of a lake.
In the middle of it
sat one boat
with one person.

Sometimes I still draw
myself like that. No longer
with pencils but with
words whispered, you
are alone.

What a shame that I forgot
somewhere along the way
that the person I drew that day
had a smile on their face.

This is just statistics

If you ever feel like you are nothing,
remember;
you are the 60.000 thoughts you have a day.
You are the 20.000 words you say
and the dreams you have
when you close your eyes.
You are all of that combined
and yet even more.

Growing pains

My heart only grew bigger
after you left.

The stars

Do the stars know we stare at them at night, thinking
life is pretty crazy,
to have put us so far away from each other looking up
to the same sky.

(all my dreams are made out of you and i.)

Do the stars know we wish upon them for our
distance to change,
thinking if only we could just fall into each other's
arms again.

(have the stars let you know that i love you so.)

Miss you

Now that I miss you, every word you say
becomes a kiss,
soft skin whispering against my ear.
Every message makes my heart skip,
the clock waiting for your return.

If someone were to take my phone
and read our conversations,
they wouldn't even begin to know
all the worlds we shared
between our late wishes, our morning hello's.

This poem is not about you

This is not a poem about the way you kissed me,
the way you totally caught me off guard
and all I wanted to say was beware
that you are holding a breaking puzzle.
This is not a poem about how the pieces fell
like mind shattering glass or how I wished
I could pick up every last one of them
and form some kind of mind control
that could produce concluding words about
how I felt. There are just no words
for a poem like that.

A picture perfect heart

You know when sometimes
a drawing can look so real
that you are unsure if it's
a drawing or a picture?

That is how I look at you,
trying to figure out if you
stepped out of a book
or were born into this world.
How do you hold your words together
like that? It is as if you
have a frame around your heart.

Missing you

Crazy little thing called life,
with the stars in the sky
and the why of it all.

Crazy big living
in the universe of
missing you.

What a mess (good story)

I dreamt that I was kissing you.
You said: "I didn't know you liked girls."
I replied: "I didn't know either, until I met you."
I woke up thinking I wish it were that simple.

But my mind falls asleep in different arms each night,
my heart so lost I don't even know who it beats for.
If love were a song, someone forgot to inform me of
the lyrics and as
a sad melody sings me to sleep,
I wish I could write a poem about my feelings and
hand it to her, run away
as she reads it.
Sneak back to see if she smiles
at the wonky lines, the crossed out words.

Good story, she'd say. I know the way her voice
would sound.
And still I can't.

The kind of notes I'd leave around our house #2

I can talk to you all day and
still feel like I want to tell you more.
So when I run out of things to say,
I'll write you an entire new universe.
We will always have stories to share.

The kind of notes I'd leave around our house #3

If love was a waiting game,
we'd win because I am patient
and you are the time flying by.

The power of a song

The flowers are back in the sky
and all of the questions of why have been answered.
Who knew that it took so little to lead up to?
This might be temporary, a band-aid
on a bleeding heart, but it is a start.
Who knew that it could be so simple?
One song and I am sold.

www.secretmidnightpress.com